Ov
Old Testament

PARTICIPANT'S BOOK

12 7s + / 110 ave

109 st close to bridge

Stephen J. Binz

Little Rock Scripture Study

THE LITURGICAL PRESS

St. John's Abbey
Collegeville, Minnesota 56321

DIOCESE OF LITTLE ROCK
2415 North Tyler Street
P.O. Box 7239, Forest Park Station
LITTLE ROCK, ARKANSAS 72217

Telephone
Area Code 501
664-0340

Office of the Bishop

Dear Friends in Christ,

I commend you for your commitment to the study of sacred Scripture. Our tradition has always insisted that the Bible is foundational for our relationship with God. It must be at the heart of our teaching, worship, and practice as followers of Christ.

St. Jerome proclaimed, "Ignorance of Scripture is ignorance of Christ." Studying the Scriptures enables us to know Christ, to share our faith with our neighbors, and to pass on that faith to the next generation.

The Bible is the Word of God in human words. So the more we can understand its history, its language, and its literary forms, the more we can understand the revelation of God to us. For we know in faith that the same Holy Spirit who inspired the Scriptures also works within us as we read and study the Bible as God's Church.

This video-based course will help you understand the Bible better. It will show you how to read the Bible, not only for information, but to experience the living presence of God in every aspect of your life.

Your friend,

+ Andrew J. McDonald

✛Andrew J. McDonald
Bishop of Little Rock

CONTENTS

Introduction

Like looking at an old family album, *Overview of the Old Testament* is an opportunity to experience a general survey of the Jewish Scriptures. It will provide you with a broad outline of the history of God's people through the ages and a general introduction to the content and themes of the biblical books. It will help you understand the types of literature found in the Scriptures, the context of the writings in the ancient Middle East, and how to connect your own life to our ancient past.

For experienced Bible users, this study will connect those parts of the Bible already studied with the whole of salvation history. For Bible beginners, it will be like looking at a map before setting out on the journey of Bible study. For all participants, this overview will whet your appetite and provide a context for ongoing reading and study of the Scriptures

The program takes an experiential approach to learning consisting of prayer, home study, group discussion, and taped lectures. It is designed to be used with a group of people who will provide encouragement, support, and shared insight for one another. Through listening, reflecting, praying, and conversing, you will come to a fuller understanding of the living Word of God.

Elements of the Program

PRAYER

Prayer is an integral part of a faith-filled study of the Bible. Each weekly session begins with a prayer service. The service is designed to encourage the group to reflect on some aspect of the Bible to be studied in the lesson to follow. The prayer helps you open your mind and heart to God's word, frees you from distractions, and helps you focus on the Scriptures.

You are also encouraged to pray privately during the week before and after you read the Bible. Reading Scripture is an opportunity to listen to God who loves you. Pray that the same Holy Spirit who inspired the Scriptures will guide you to correctly understand what you read and empower you to make what you read a part of your life.

PERSONAL STUDY

Between each session you are encouraged to study the Bible at home. The only resources you need are a modern translation of the Bible and this Participant's Book. You will find questions in this book to guide your home study. Space is provided for writing your responses to each question.

The home study continues to explore the information given in the weekly lectures. Some questions will deepen your understanding of what you learned; others will anticipate the material you will learn in the next lecture. Many questions will synthesize the elements learned from the program and encourage a personal application of the Scriptures to your contemporary life.

Daily prayer, reading, and study of the Bible is a good habit to establish. Writing your responses will help you organize and clarify your thoughts.

GROUP DISCUSSION

Your written responses to the questions for home study will form the basis of the weekly group discussion. The discussion allows you to grow in your understanding as you share insights with others in the group. You will begin to build a supportive community that encourages one another to continue daily reflection on the Scriptures.

TAPED LECTURES

The informational content of this program will be provided through a series of lectures on video tape. These lectures are outlined in this book so that you will be able to follow along and add your own notes if you wish.

The first two lectures will help you understand the Pentateuch, the foundational writings of the Hebrew Scriptures. The lectures will explore the creation accounts, the stories of the patriarchs, the exodus event, and formation of the covenant in the wilderness.

Lectures three and four will survey ancient history from the point of view of the Bible's historical books. The lectures will discuss Israel's history from the entry into the Promised Land, through the judges, monarchy, exile, and restoration.

The fifth and sixth lecture will discuss the great variety of Israel's other writings. Poetry, songs, short stories, proverbs, and other wisdom writings fill many books of the Bible's Jewish literature.

The prophetic literature of Israel is the subject of lectures seven and eight. The prophets of Israel challenge the kings and priests, promote justice in the land, urge Israel to return to the covenant, and proclaim God's future deeds of salvation.

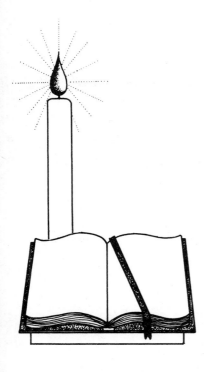

SCHEDULE FOR <u>FOUR</u> WEEKLY SESSIONS

Week 1   Date: _____

Prayer Service: "The Journey to Freedom and Life"   p. 11
Lecture 1   p. 28
Discussion Questions 1-6   p. 74
Lecture 2   p. 33
Closing
Personal Study—Complete Questions 7–12   p. 78

Week 2   Date: _____

Prayer Service: "Saving History Is Our History"   p. 15
Lecture 3   p. 39
Discussion Questions 7-12   p. 78
Lecture 4   p. 45
Closing
Personal Study—Complete Questions 13–18   p. 84

Week 3   Date: _____

Prayer Service: "Stories and Songs of God's Goodness"   p. 19
Lecture 5   p. 53
Discussion Questions 13-18   p. 84
Lecture 6   p. 57
Closing
Personal Study—Complete Questions 19–24   p. 90

Week 4   Date: _____

Prayer Service: "The Prophetic Call to Justice"   p. 23
Lecture 7   p. 61
Discussion Questions 19-24   p. 90
Lecture 8   p. 67
Closing

SCHEDULE FOR EIGHT WEEKLY SESSIONS

Week 1   Date: _____

Prayer Service: "The Journey to Freedom and Life"   p. 11
Lecture 1 p. 28
Discussion Questions 1-3 p. 74
Closing

Personal Study—Complete Questions 4–6 p. 76

Week 2   Date: _____

Prayer Service: "Bonded with God in Covenant"   p. 13
Lecture 2 p. 33
Discussion Questions 4-6 p. 76
Closing

Personal Study—Complete Questions 7–9 p. 78

Week 3   Date: _____

Prayer Service: "Saving History Is Our History"   p. 15
Lecture 3 p. 39
Discussion Questions 7-9 p. 78
Closing

Personal Study—Complete Questions 10–12 p. 80

Week 4   Date: _____

Prayer Service: "God's Reign Is Everlasting"   p. 17
Lecture 4 p. 45
Discussion Questions 10-12 p. 80
Closing

Personal Study—Complete Questions 13–15 p. 84

Week 5   Date: _____

Prayer Service: "Stories and Songs of God's Goodness"   p. 19
Lecture 5   p. 53
Discussion Questions 13-15   p. 84
Closing
Personal Study—Complete Questions 16–18   p. 86

Week 6   Date: _____

Prayer Service: "All Wisdom Comes from God"   p. 21
Lecture 6   p. 57
Discussion Questions 16-18   p. 86
Closing
Personal Study—Complete Questions 19–21   p. 90

Week 7   Date: _____

Prayer Service: "The Prophetic Call to Justice"   p. 23
Lecture 7   p. 61
Discussion Questions 19-21   p. 90
Closing
Personal Study—Complete Questions 22–24   p. 92

Week 8   Date: _____

Prayer Service: "Entrust Your Future to God"   p. 25
Lecture 8   p. 67
Discussion Questions 22-24   p. 92
Closing

The Journey to Freedom and Life

Leader: O God, our Creator, you revealed yourself to our ancestors and called them to trust in you. You call each of us
to follow you along the journey of our fathers and mothers
of faith. Give us courage and a willingness to trust in your
guidance and rely on your strength as we travel from
slavery and death to freedom and life.

Reader: *Exodus 3:11-17*

Response: *Psalm 136:1, 4-16, 21-22, 26*

Leader: Praise the LORD, who is so good;
All: God's love endures forever;

Leader: Who alone has done great wonders,
All: God's love endures forever;

Leader: Who skillfully made the heavens,
All: God's love endures forever;

Leader: Who spread the earth upon the waters,
All: God's love endures forever;

Leader: Who made the great lights,
All: God's love endures forever;

Leader: The sun to rule the day,
All: God's love endures forever;

Leader: The moon and stars to rule the night,
All: God's love endures forever;

Leader: Who struck down the firstborn of Egypt,
All: God's love endures forever;

Leader: And led Israel from their midst,
All: God's love endures forever;

Leader: With mighty hand and outstretched arm,
All: God's love endures forever;

Leader: Who split in two the Red Sea,
All: God's love endures forever;

Leader: And led Israel through,
All: God's love endures forever;

Leader: But swept Pharaoh and his army into the Red Sea,
All: God's love endures forever;

Leader: Who led the people through the desert,
All: God's love endures forever;

Leader: And made their lands a heritage
All: God's love endures forever;

Leader: A heritage for Israel, God's servant,
All: God's love endures forever;

Leader: Praise the God of heaven,
All: God's love endures forever.

Leader: O God, our Liberator, you freed your people from slavery and led them to the mountain of your covenant. Deliver us from all that enslaves us and prevents us from being the people you have called us to be. Help us to free one another from the chains of fear, hopelessness, and despair.

Leader: Lord, you have made us your chosen people.

All: Help us to live worthy of your call.

Leader: You have made us a kingdom of priests.

All: Help us to offer our life in your service.

Leader: You have made us a holy people.

All: Help us to live honorably in your presence. Amen.

Bonded with God in Covenant

Leader: Liberating God, what wonders you work to free your people from bondage! You lead us through the wilderness so that we may serve you in freedom. Help us to experience the intimacy of your covenant bond so that we may respond to your law with love.

Reader: *Exodus 19:3-8*

Response: *Psalm 114*

Left: When Israel came forth from Egypt,
   the house of Jacob from an alien people,
Judah became God's holy place,
   Israel, God's domain.

Right: The sea beheld and fled;
   the Jordan turned back.
The mountains skipped like rams;
   the hills, like lambs of the flock.

Left: Why was it, sea, that you fled?
   Jordan, that you turned back?
You mountains, that you skipped like rams?
   You hills, like lambs of the flock?

Right: Tremble, earth, before the Lord,
   before the God of Jacob,
Who turned rocks into pools of water,
   stones into flowing springs.

Leader: Release us, Lord, from the captivity of sin and guilt.

All: "Let my people go that they might serve me."

Leader: Release us, Lord, from servitude to money and possessions.

All: "Let my people go that they might serve me."

Leader: Release us, Lord, from the bondage of addictions and destructive habits.

All: "Let my people go that they might serve me."

Leader: Lift us up, O God, as an eagle carries its young through the skies. Help us to serve you in covenant so that we can know the genuine freedom of your people.

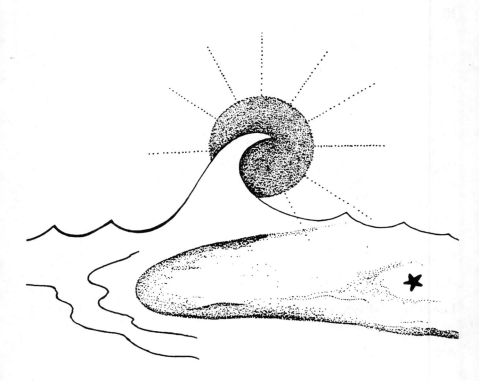

Saving History Is Our History

Leader: God our Savior, you fulfill your promises to us in ways that exceed our expectations. Generation after generation proclaim the great deeds you have done in their midst. In the bond of covenant you care for our every need and challenge us to care for the needs of one another. May the actions of our lives be a response to your abundant goodness to us, so that we may be signs of your saving will for all people.

Reader: Let us listen to the account from the Book of Joshua as the people recommit themselves to the covenant in the promised land of Israel.

Joshua 8:30-35

Response: *Psalm 105:1-2, 6-11, 26-27, 38-45*

Left: Give thanks to the LORD, invoke his name;
     make known among the peoples his deeds!
Sing praise, play music;
     proclaim all his wondrous deeds!

Right: You descendants of Abraham his servant,
     offspring of Jacob, the chosen one!
The LORD is our God
     who rules the whole earth.

Left: He remembers forever his covenant,
     the pact imposed for a thousand generations,
Which was made with Abraham,
     confirmed by oath to Isaac,

Right: And ratified as binding for Jacob,
     an everlasting covenant for Israel:
"To you I give the land of Canaan,
     your own allotted heritage."

Left: He sent his servant Moses,
     Aaron whom he had chosen.

They worked his signs in Egypt
and wonders in the land of Ham.

Right: Egypt rejoiced when they left,
for panic had seized them.
He spread a cloud as a cover,
and made a fire to light up the night.

Left: They asked and he brought them quail;
with bread from heaven he filled them.
He split the rock and water gushed forth;
it flowed through the desert like a river.

Right: For he remembered his sacred word
to Abraham his servant.
He brought his people out with joy,
his chosen ones with shouts of triumph.

Left: He gave them the lands of the nations,
the wealth of the peoples to own,
That they might keep his laws
and observe his teachings.
Hallelujah!

Leader: Lord, out of all the people of the earth, you have called us to be your own.

All: You are our God and we are your people.

Leader: You brought us to a land flowing with milk and honey.

All: You are our God and we are your people.

Leader: Around the altar of sacrifice your people committed their lives to you.

All: You are our God and we are your people.

Leader: The Lord bless you and keep you! The Lord let his face shine upon you, and be gracious to you! The Lord look upon you kindly and give you peace! *(Num 6:24-26)*

All: Amen.

God's Reign Is Everlasting

Leader: God our King, you established your kingdom with the nation of Israel and you extend your reign to all the earth. We want to make our lives and our land a worthy dwelling place for you. May all people experience the justice and compassion of your kingdom and may your rule lead to lasting peace.

Reader: Let us listen to this account of King Solomon as he concluded the dedication of the temple of Jerusalem.

1 Kings 8:54-63

Response: *Psalm 132:7-18*

Left: Let us enter God's dwelling;
    let us worship at God's footstool.
Arise, LORD, come to your resting place,
    you and your majestic ark.

Right: Your priests will be clothed with justice;
    your faithful will shout for joy.
For the sake of David your servant,
    do not reject your anointed.

Left: The LORD swore an oath to David,
    a pledge never to be broken:
"Your own offspring I will set upon your throne.

Right: If your sons observe my covenant,
    the laws I shall teach them,
Their sons, in turn,
    shall sit forever on your throne."

Left: Yes, the LORD has chosen Zion,
    desired it for a dwelling:
"This is my resting place forever;
    here I will dwell, for I desire it.

Right: I will bless Zion with meat;
its poor I will fill with bread.
I will clothe its priests with blessing;
its faithful shall shout for joy.

Left: There I will make a horn sprout for David's line;
I will set a lamp for my anointed.
His foes I will clothe with shame,
but on him my crown shall gleam."

Leader: Lord, give your peace to all the nations and peoples of the world.

All: May your kingdom come, your will be done.

Leader: Heal the sick and restore all those afflicted and in distress.

All: May your kingdom come, your will be done.

Leader: Give guidance and wisdom to all those in authority in your Church and in your world.

All: May your kingdom come, your will be done.

Leader: Let us pray for the coming of God's kingdom as Jesus taught us.

All: Our Father . . .

Stories and Songs of God's Goodness

Leader: Loving and merciful God, you choose women and men to declare your goodness generation after generation. Through songs and stories, liturgies and feasts, your people proclaim and celebrate your wonders in their midst. Through the stories of your people and the songs of our faith, help us to trust in your goodness and be assured of your loving presence with us in every age.

Reader: Let us listen to the Book of Ruth in which God gives a child to Ruth and the people proclaim God's goodness to her mother-in-law Naomi.

Ruth 4:13-17

Response: *Judith 13:18-20; 15:9-10*

Leader: Blessed are you, daughter, by the Most High God, above all the women on earth; and blessed be the LORD God, the creator of heaven and earth.

All: You are the glory of Jerusalem, the surpassing joy of Israel; you are the splendid boast of our people.

Leader: Your deed of hope will never be forgotten by those who tell of the might of God.

All: You are the glory of Jerusalem, the surpassing joy of Israel; you are the splendid boast of our people.

Leader: May God make this redound to your everlasting honor, rewarding you with blessings, because you risked your life when your people were being oppressed, and you averted our disaster, walking uprightly before our God.

All: You are the glory of Jerusalem, the surpassing joy of Israel; you are the splendid boast of our people.

Leader: With your own hand you have done all this;
　　　　 you have done good to Israel,
　　　　 and God is pleased with what you have wrought.

May you be blessed by the LORD Almighty
forever and ever!

All: You are the glory of Jerusalem, the surpassing joy of Israel; you are the splendid boast of our people.

All: How good to celebrate our God in song;
how sweet to give fitting praise.
The LORD rebuilds Jerusalem,
gathers the dispersed of Israel,
Heals the brokenhearted,
binds up their wounds,
Numbers all the stars,
calls each of them by name.
Great is our Lord, vast in power,
with wisdom beyond measure. *(Ps 147:1-5)*

All Wisdom Comes from God

Leader: Generous God, you are the source of all good gifts. We thank you for your gifts of wisdom and understanding. Increase your gifts within us so that we can know your word, love your ways, and follow your will. Help us to accept the limits of our human knowledge and give us a reverence for your perfect and inscrutable wisdom so that we may trust in you always.

Reader: Let us listen to the wisdom of Sirach as he praises the wisdom of God.

Sirach 1:1-11

Response: *Psalm 34:2-19*

Left: I will bless the Lord at all times;
 praise shall be always in my mouth.
My soul will glory in the LORD
 that the poor may hear and be glad.

Right: Magnify the LORD with me;
 let us exalt his name together.
I sought the LORD, who answered me,
 delivered me from all my fears.

Left: Look to God that you may be radiant with joy
 and your faces may not blush for shame.
In my misfortune I called,
 the LORD heard and saved me from all distress.

Right: The angel of the LORD, who encamps with them,
 delivers all who fear God.
Learn to savor how good the LORD is;
 happy are those who take refuge in him.

Left: Fear the LORD, you holy ones;
 nothing is lacking to those who fear him.
The powerful grow poor and hungry,
 but those who seek the LORD lack no good thing.

Right: Come, children, listen to me;
    I will teach you the fear of the LORD.
   Who among you loves life,
    takes delight in prosperous days?

Left: Keep your tongue from evil,
    your lips from speaking lies.
   Turn from evil and do good;
    seek peace and pursue it.

Right: The LORD has eyes for the just
    and ears for their cry.
   The LORD's face is against evildoers
    to wipe out their memory from the earth.

Left: When the just cry out, the LORD hears
    and rescues them from all distress.
   The LORD is close to the brokenhearted,
    saves those whose spirit is crushed.

Leader: God's wisdom proclaims that life is not a burden to be borne but a gift to be shared.

All: "Happy are all who fear the LORD,
    who walk in the ways of God."

Leader: God's wisdom proclaims that suffering is not a curse from God but a means to growth.

All: "Happy are all who fear the LORD,
    who walk in the ways of God."

Leader: God's wisdom proclaims that death is not an utter abyss but the beginning of eternal reward.

All: "Happy are all who fear the LORD,
    who walk in the ways of God."

The Prophetic Call to Justice

Leader: God of peace and justice, you hear the poor who call upon you, and you save the needy and neglected. Your word challenges us to confront the attitudes and institutions that prevent the coming of your reign. Give us the insight and the passion of your prophets so that we may hear your word and do your will. Let your peace and your justice come upon our land.

Reader: Let us listen as the prophet Micah proclaims the peace of God's future reign.

Micah 4:1-3

Response: *Psalm 72:1-4, 11-14, 17*

Left: O God, give your judgment to the king;
    your justice to the son of kings;
That he may govern your people with justice,
    your oppressed with right judgment,

Right: That the mountains may yield their bounty for the people,
    and the hills great abundance,
That he may defend the oppressed among the people,
    save the poor and crush the oppressor.

Left: May all kings bow before him,
    all nations serve him.
For he rescues the poor when they cry out,
    the oppressed who have no one to help.

Right: He shows pity to the needy and the poor
    and saves the lives of the poor.
From extortion and violence he frees them,
    for precious is their blood in his sight.

Left: May his name be blessed forever;
    as long as the sun, may his name endure.
May the tribes of the earth give blessings with his name;
    may all the nations regard him as favored.

Leader: Just and merciful God, teach us to share our bread with the hungry and to shelter the homeless poor.

All: Lord, make me an instrument of your peace.

Leader: Give us the conviction do seek justice in our land by playing an active role in the institutions of our society.

All: Lord, make me an instrument of your peace.

Leader: Convert our hearts and our lives so that we may do justice, love goodness, and walk humbly in your sight.

All: Lord, make me an instrument of your peace.
Where there is hatred let me sow love;
   where there is injury, pardon;
   where there is doubt, faith;
   where there is despair, hope;
   where there is darkness, light; and
   where there is sadness, joy.

O divine Master, grant that I may not so much seek
   to be consoled as to console,
   to be understood as to understand,
   to be loved as to love.
For it is in giving that we receive,
   it is in pardoning that we are pardoned; and
   it is in dying that we are born to eternal life.

Entrust Your Future to God

Leader: God of the past, present, and future, in every age you are faithful to your people. As we learn the history of our salvation, you fill our lives with promises of the future. As our ancestors trusted in you, help us to rely on you and look to the future with expectation, confident in your everlasting covenant and your loving promises.

Reader: Let us listen to the prophet Isaiah as he proclaims the good things to come.

Isaiah 61:1-3

Response: *The Prophet Isaiah*

Left: They that hope in the LORD will renew their strength,
    they will soar as with eagles' wings;
They will run and not grow weary,
    walk and not grow faint. *(40:31)*

Right: Fear not, I am with you;
    be not dismayed; I am your God.
I will strengthen you, and help you,
    and uphold you with my right hand of justice. *(41:10)*

Left: I, the LORD, have called you for the victory of justice,
    I have grasped you by the hand;
I have formed you, and set you
    as a covenant of the people,
    a light for the nations. *(42:6)*

Right: I will lead the blind on their journey;
    by paths unknown I will guide them.
I will turn darkness into light before them,
    and make crooked ways straight. *(42:16)*

Left: When you pass through the water, I will be with you;
    in the rivers you shall not drown.
When you walk through fire, you shall not be burned;
    the flames shall not consume you. *(43:2)*

Right: Remember not the events of the past,
           the things of long ago consider not;
      See, I am doing something new!
           Now it springs forth, do you not perceive it? *(43:18-19)*

Left: I will pour out water upon the thirsty ground,
           and streams upon the dry land;
       I will pour out my spirit upon your offspring,
           and my blessing upon your descendants. *(44:3)*

Right: Let justice descend, O heavens, like dew from above,
           like gentle rain let the skies drop it down.
      Let the earth open and salvation bud forth;
           let justice also spring up! *(45:8)*

Left: I am bringing on my justice, it is not far off,
           my salvation shall not tarry;
       I will put salvation within Zion,
           and give to Israel my glory. *(46:13)*

Right: Sing out, O heavens, and rejoice, O earth,
           break forth into song, you mountains.
      For the LORD comforts his people
           and shows mercy to his afflicted. *(49:13)*

Left: Can a mother forget her infant,
           be without tenderness for the child of her womb?
       Even should she forget,
           I will never forget you. *(49:15)*

Right: Though the mountains leave their place
           and the hills be shaken,
      My love shall never leave you
           nor my covenant of peace be shaken. *(54:10)*

Left: Yes, in joy you shall depart,
           in peace you shall be brought back;
       Mountains and hills shall break out in song before you,
           and all the trees of the countryside shall clap their
           hands. *(55:12)*

Right: Lo, I am about to create new heavens
and a new earth;
The things of the past shall not be remembered
or come to mind. *(65:17)*

All: You are my hope, Lord,
my trust, GOD, from my youth.
On you I depend since birth;
from my mother's womb you are my strength;
my hope in you never wavers. *(Ps 71:5-6)*

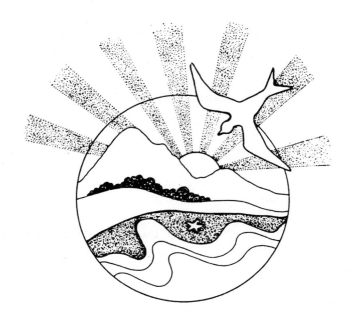

LECTURE 1—THE PENTATEUCH: ISRAEL'S BEGINNINGS

I.   Introduction—An Overview of the Bible

II.   The Pentateuch—The Torah

III. The Book of Genesis

   A. Gen 1–11

      1. Truths taught by the creation account of Genesis 1

         a. There is one God.

         b. God is the cause of all that exists.

         c. The sun and moon are not gods.

         d. All creation is good.

         e. People are especially good.

         f. Men and women are equally made in the image of a loving God.

         g. Men and women are co-creators and stewards of the earth.

      2. Truths taught by the account of Adam and Eve

         a. Human beings are created by God with free will.

         b. The root cause of human suffering is sin.

    c. Sin disrupts human relationships and brings about shame and blame.

    d. Suffering is not a punishment inflicted by God, but a consequence of sin.

    e. Human beings suffer from our own sin and that of others.

B. Gen 12–50

  1. God's promises to Abraham

    a. Abraham would be given a new land.

    b. Abraham's numerous descendants would form a great nation.

    c. Through Abraham, all the nations of the earth will be blessed.

  2. The descendants of Abraham and Sarah

    a. Ishmael and Isaac (married Rebekah)

    b. Esau and Jacob (married Rachel and Leah)

    c. Sons of Jacob-Israel: Reuben, Simeon, Levi, Judah, Issachar, Zebulun, Dan, Naphtali, Gad, Asher, Joseph, and Benjamin.

IV. The Book of Exodus

"Now Joseph and all his brothers and that whole generation died. But the Israelites were fruitful and prolific. They became so numer-

ous and strong that the land was filled with them. Then a new
king, who knew nothing of Joseph, came to power in Egypt."
(Exod 1:6-8)

A. Divisions of the Book of Exodus

    1. Exod 1–12—The Israelites in Egypt

    2. Exod 12–18—The exodus from Egypt and journey to Sinai

    3. Exod 19–24—The covenant at Mt. Sinai

    4. Exod 25–40—The Ark of the Covenant and the Tabernacle.

B. The Call of Moses

"I am the God of your father, the God of Abraham, the God
of Isaac, the God of Jacob. . . . I have witnessed the affliction of my people in Egypt and have heard their cry of com-
plaint against their slave drivers, so I know well what they
are suffering. Therefore I have come down to rescue them
from the hands of the Egyptians and lead them out of that
land into a good and spacious land, a land flowing with milk
and honey. . . ." *(Exod 3:6-8)*

C. The Divine Name—"Ehyeh-Asher-Ehyeh"

D. Stories of Deliverance

    1. The plagues in Egypt *(Exod 7–11)*

2. The crossing of the Sea

V. Timeline

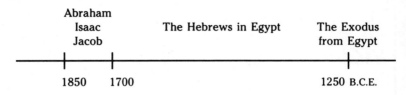

Abraham Isaac Jacob	The Hebrews in Egypt	The Exodus from Egypt
1850 1700		1250 B.C.E.

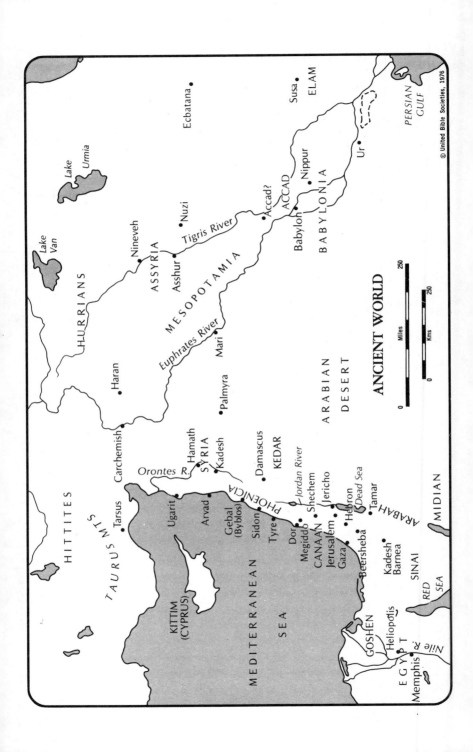

ANCIENT WORLD

LECTURE 2—THE PENTATEUCH: ISRAEL'S FOUNDATIONAL COVENANT

I.   Mount Sinai as the focus of the Pentateuch

   A. Leading toward Sinai: Genesis, Exodus 1–18

   B. At Sinai: Exodus 19–40, Leviticus, Numbers 1–10

   C. Moving from Sinai: Numbers 10–36, Deuteronomy

II. God's covenant and Israel's obedience to Torah

   "Let my people go that they might serve me."

   A. To worship God rightly.

   B. To deal justly with one another.

III. Moses as "author-ity" of Torah

IV. God's Covenant in Exodus

    A. Covenant bond is sealed through covenant sacrifice and covenant meal.

    B. The Ark of the Covenant, Tabernacle, and Priesthood

    C. Covenant unfaithfulness—the golden calf

V.   The Book of Leviticus

    A. The call to Holiness

    "You shall make and keep yourselves holy, because I am holy." *(Lev 11:44)*

    "Be holy, for I, the LORD, your God, am holy." *(Lev 19:2)*

    B. Contents of Leviticus

       1. Lev 1–7—The ritual of sacrifice

       2. Lev 8–10—The ordination ritual for priests

       3. Lev 11–16—The code of laws regarding legal purity

       4. Lev 17–26—The code of legal holiness

VI.   The Book of Numbers

A. Divisions of Numbers

   1. Num 1–10—The organization of the twelve tribes

   2. Num 10–22—The journey through the wilderness

   3. Num 22–36—The events on the Plains of Moab

B. Forty years of wandering in the wilderness

C. Temptation, murmuring, and rebellion

VII. The Book of Deuteronomy

A. The speeches of Moses

   1. Deut 1–4—Moses reviews the events from Mount Sinai to the present

   2. Deut 5–11—Moses reminds the people of the covenant

   3. Deut 12–26—Moses restates and explains the law

   4. Deut 27–34—Moses' last words and his death

B. The theme of God's love

"Hear, O Israel! The LORD is our God, the LORD alone! Therefore, you shall love the LORD, your God, with all your heart, and with all your soul, and with all your strength. Take to heart these words which I enjoin on you today. Drill them into your children. Speak of them at home and abroad, whether you are busy or at rest. Bind them at your wrist as a sign and let them be as a pendant on your forehead. Write them on the doorposts of your houses and on your gates." *(Deut 6:4-9)*

C. "Remembering" makes the covenant present for every generation

"The LORD, our God, made a covenant with us at Horeb; not with our fathers did he make this covenant, but with us, all of us who are alive here this day." *(Deut 5:2-3)*

"This day the LORD, your God, commands you to observe these statutes and decrees. Be careful, then, to observe them with all your heart and with all your soul. Today you are making this agreement with the LORD." *(Deut 26:16-17a)*

D. The choice before God's people

"This is why you must know, and fix in your heart, that the LORD is God in the heavens above and on earth below, and that there is no other." *(Deut 4:39)*

"I have set before you life and death, the blessing and the curse. Choose life, then, that you and your descendants may live, by loving the LORD, your God, heeding his voice, and holding fast to him. For that will mean life for you, a long life for you to live on the land which the LORD swore he would give to your fathers Abraham, Isaac, and Jacob." *(Deut 30:19-20)*

VIII. The Pentateuch establishes Israel's identity

    A. Genesis shows us Israel's origins.

    B. Exodus shows us Israel's birth as a people.

    C. Leviticus describes the holy nature of Israel.

    D. Numbers describes the organization of Israel.

    E. Deuteronomy shows us the spirit of Israel.

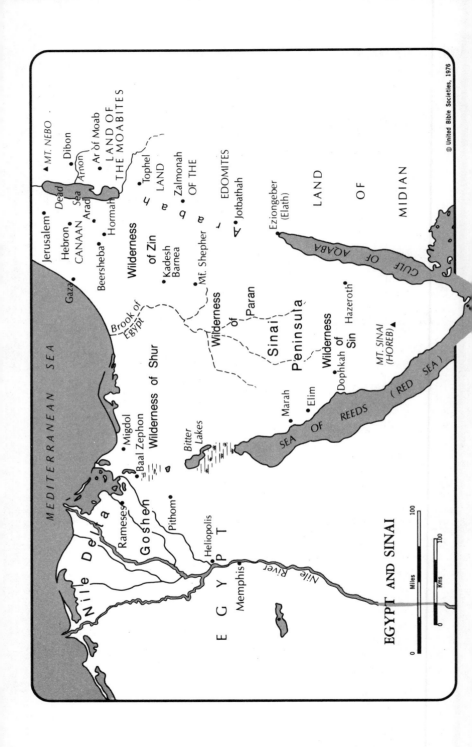

EGYPT AND SINAI

© United Bible Societies, 1976

LECTURE 3—THE HISTORICAL BOOKS: FROM CONQUEST TO KINGDOM

I. The Deuteronomist History (Joshua, Judges, 1 and 2 Samuel, and 1 and 2 Kings)

    A. From the death of Moses (1210 B.C.E.) to the destruction of Jerusalem (587 B.C.E.)

    B. Israel's choice between life and death, the blessing and the curse

II. The Book of Joshua

    A. The conquest of Canaan *(Josh 1–12)*

       "Thus Joshua captured the whole country, just as the LORD had foretold to Moses. Joshua gave it to Israel as their heritage, apportioning it among the tribes. And the land enjoyed peace." *(Josh 11:23)*

    B. The division of the land *(Josh 13–21)*

    C. Joshua's farewell and renewal of the covenant *(Josh 22–24)*

       "Now, therefore, fear the LORD and serve him completely and sincerely. . . If it does not please you to serve the LORD, decide today whom you will serve. . . As for me and my household, we will serve the LORD." *(Josh 24:14-15)*

III.   The Book of Judges

    A. The cycle of sin, punishment, repentance, deliverance

    B. A loose confederation of the twelve tribes

       "In those days there was no king in Israel; everyone did what he thought best." *(Judg 21:25)*

IV.   The Books of First and Second Samuel

    A. Samuel—judge, priest, and prophet

    B. Pro-monarchy and anti-monarchy

    C. Saul—Israel's first king

    D. God's choice of David—Israel's ideal king

       "Not as man sees does God see, because man sees the appearance but the LORD looks into the heart." *(1 Sam 16:7)*

    E. Divisions of First Samuel

1. 1 Sam 1–7—The judgeship of Samuel and the oppression by the Philistines

2. 1 Sam 8–15—The people's demand for a king and the rise and fall of Saul

3. 1 Sam 16–31—David's early life and the death of Saul.

F. Divisions of Second Samuel

1. 2 Sam 1–4—David's early reign in Judah

2. 2 Sam 5–20—The kingship of David

3. 2 Sam 21–24—Appendix of documents about David

G. David's greatest accomplishments

1. David captured the city of Jerusalem and made it the capital of the kingdom.

2. David decisively defeated the Philistines.

3. David brought the Ark of the Covenant to Jerusalem.

H. God's covenant with David

"The LORD also reveals to you that he will establish a house for you. And when your time comes and you rest with your ancestors, I will raise up your heir after you, sprung from your loins, and I will make his kingdom firm. It is he who shall build a house for my name. And I will make his royal throne firm forever. I will be a father to him, and he shall be a son to me. . . . Your house and your kingdom shall endure forever before me; your throne shall stand firm forever." *(2 Sam 7:11-14, 16)*

V. Timeline

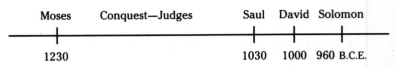

DIVISION OF CANAAN

Miles 0 — 40

Kms 0 — 40

Sidon

SIDONIANS

LEBANON MTS.

HITTITES

ARAMEANS

Damascus

▲ MT. HERMON

Tyre

DAN

Dan (Laish)

ASHER

NAPHTALI

Hazor

MEDITERRANEAN

MANASSEH (EAST)

Ashtaroth

SEA

MT. CARMEL ▲

Lake Galilee

ZEBULUN

MT. TABOR ▲

Dor

Megiddo

Endor

Shunem

ISSACHAR

Jezreel

MT. GILBOA ▲

Ramoth

MANASSEH (WEST)

Jordan River

Jabesh

Shechem

GAD

AMMONITES

Joppa

Shiloh

EPHRAIM

Bethel

Gilgal

DAN

Ai

BENJAMIN

Jericho

Rabbah

Gibeah

Ashdod

Jerusalem

Bethpeor

Libnah

Ashkelon

Bethlehem

REUBEN

Gath?

Lachish

JUDAH

Hebron

Dead

Gaza

PHILISTINES

Engedi

Sea

Gath?

Beersheba

Hormah

MOABITES

SIMEON

The Negev

EDOMITES

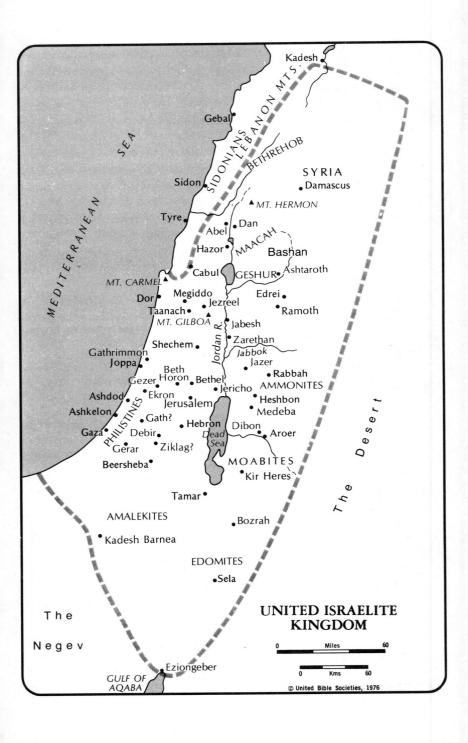

UNITED ISRAELITE
KINGDOM

Solomon's sin → power lust wealth

LECTURE 4—THE HISTORICAL BOOKS: DIVISION, EXILE, AND RESTORATION

I. Functions of Israel's Kings

   A. Military

   B. Legal

   C. Religious

II. The Reign of Solomon

   A. The gift of wisdom

      "O LORD, my God, you have made me, your servant, king to succeed my father David; but I am a mere youth, not knowing at all how to act. I serve you in the midst of the people whom you have chosen, a people so vast that it cannot be numbered or counted. Give your servant, therefore, an understanding heart to judge your people and to distinguish right from wrong." *(1 Kgs 3:7-9)*

   B. Important accomplishments

      1. He divided the kingdom into twelve administrative districts.

      2. He developed a powerful corp of horsemen and chariots.

3. He built a magnificent palace for his royal court.

4. He constructed a defensive wall around Jerusalem.

5. He built fortress cities for arms and supplies.

6. He established Israel as a center for learning and the arts.

7. He established the kingdom as a center for trade.

C. Solomon's construction of the Temple

1. Structure

2. Expression of the covenant

" . . . the place which the LORD, your God, chooses out of all your tribes and designates as his dwelling." *(Deut 12:5)*

3. Mediation of God's presence

"Can it indeed be that God dwells among men on earth? If the heavens and the highest heavens cannot contain you, how much less this temple which I have built. . . . May your eyes watch night and day over this temple, the place where you have decreed you shall be honored; may you heed the prayer which I, your servant, offer in this place. Listen to the petitions of your servant and of your people Israel which they offer in this place. Listen from your heavenly dwelling and grant pardon." *(1 Kgs 8:27, 29-30)*

D. The decline of Solomon's reign

"He shall not have a great number of horses; nor shall he make his people go back again to Egypt to acquire them. . . . Neither shall he have a great number of wives, lest his heart be estranged, nor shall he accumulate a vast amount of silver and gold." *(Deut 17:16-17)*

III. Division of the Kingdom

    A. Northern tribes, hereafter called Israel.

       1. Jeroboam I as king

       2. Religious shrines at Dan and Bethel

       3. Destruction by Assyria in 721 B.C.E.

    B. Southern tribes, hereafter called Judah.

       1. Rehoboam continues the line of David in Jerusalem

       2. King Hezekiah (715 to 687 B.C.E.) and Josiah (640 to 609 B.C.E.)

       3. Fall to Babylon in 587 B.C.E.

IV. The Books of First and Second Kings

    A. 1 Kgs 1–11—reign of King Solomon.

B. 1 Kgs 12–2 Kgs 17—parallel histories of the northern and southern kingdoms to the destruction of Israel by Assyria.

C. 2 Kgs 18–27—last kings of Judah until the fall of Jerusalem and the exile to Babylon.

V.   Timeline

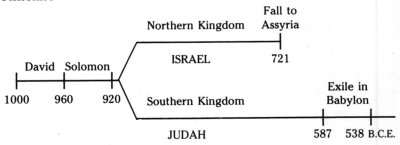

VI.   The Period of Exile

A. Suffering, purification, and renewal

B. Collecting traditions and editing the Scriptures

VII.   The Period of Restoration

A. The decree of King Cyrus of Persia

"Thus says Cyrus, king of Persia: 'All the kingdoms of the earth
the LORD, the God of heaven, has given to me, and he has
also charged me to build him a house in Jerusalem, which
is in Judah. Whoever, therefore, among you belongs to any
part of his people, let him go up, and may his God be with
him! Let everyone who has survived, in whatever place he
may have dwelt, be assisted by the people of that place with
silver, gold, goods, and cattle, together with free-will offer-
ings for the house of God in Jerusalem.'" *(Ezra 1:2-4)*

B. Rebuilding Jerusalem and the Temple

C. Restoring observance of the Torah

VIII. The Work of the Chronicler

A. 1 and 2 Chron—Salvation history with a focus on David and
the temple

B. Ezra 1–6—Return and resettlement of the first exiles followed
by the rebuilding of the altar and the temple

C. Ezra 7–10—Return of Ezra and a second group of exiles and
the reforms of Ezra

D. Neh 1–7—Return of Nehemiah, the rebuilding of Jerusalem's walls, and the census of the people

E. Neh 8–13—Renewal of the covenant and the religious reforms instituted by Ezra and Nehemiah

IX.   Maccabean Revolt

A. Jewish persecution under Antiochus IV

B. Jewish revolt under Mattathias and his five sons

C. Recapture and rededication of the Temple

D. 1 and 2 Maccabees

X.   Timeline

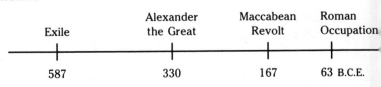

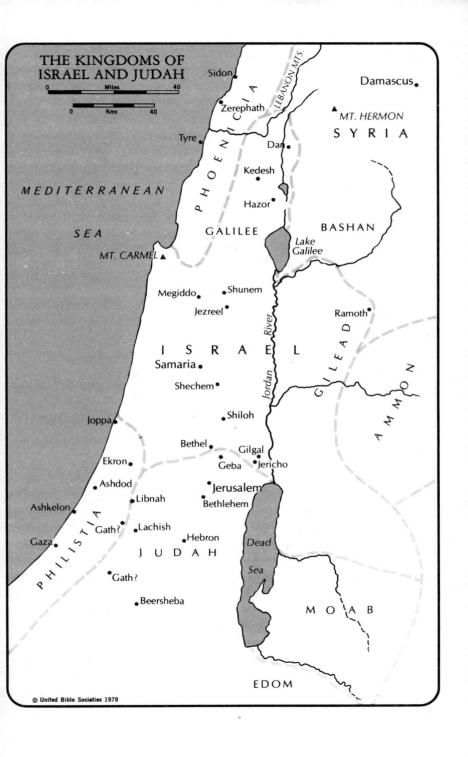

THE KINGDOMS OF
ISRAEL AND JUDAH

Miles 0 · 40

Kms 0 · 40

MEDITERRANEAN

SEA

Sidon

Zerephath

Tyre

PHOENICIA

LEBANON MTS.

Damascus

MT. HERMON

SYRIA

Dan

Kedesh

Hazor

GALILEE

BASHAN

Lake Galilee

MT. CARMEL

Megiddo

Shunem

Jezreel

Ramoth

GILEAD

I S R A E L

Samaria

Shechem

Jordan River

AMMON

Joppa

Shiloh

Bethel

Gilgal

Geba

Jericho

Ekron

Jerusalem

Ashdod

Bethlehem

Ashkelon

Libnah

PHILISTIA

Gath?

Lachish

Gaza

Hebron

J U D A H

Dead

Sea

Gath?

Beersheba

M O A B

EDOM

© United Bible Societies 1978

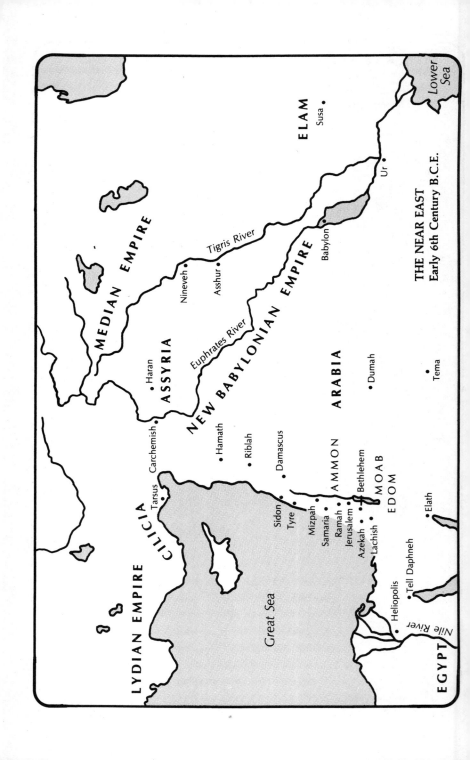

THE NEAR EAST
Early 6th Century B.C.E.

Lower Sea

ELAM
Susa

MEDIAN EMPIRE

Tigris River

Nineveh
Asshur
Babylon
Ur

Euphrates River

ASSYRIA

Haran

NEW BABYLONIAN EMPIRE

ARABIA

Dumah
Tema

Hamath
Riblah
Damascus

AMMON

Bethlehem
MOAB
EDOM
Elath

CILICIA

Tarsus
Carchemish

Sidon
Tyre
Mizpah
Samaria
Ramah
Jerusalem
Azekah
Lachish
Tell Daphneh

LYDIAN EMPIRE

Great Sea

Heliopolis
Nile River

EGYPT

LECTURE 5—THE WRITINGS:
ISRAEL'S SHORT STORIES AND SONGS

I.   The Short Stories

   A. The Book of Ruth

      "Do not ask me to abandon or forsake you! for wherever you
      go I will go, wherever you lodge I will lodge, your people shall
      be my people, and your God my God." *(1:16)*

   B. The Book of Tobit

   C. The Book of Judith

      "You are the glory of Jerusalem, the surpassing joy of Israel;
      you are the splendid boast of our people." *(15:9)*

   D. The Book of Esther

   E. The Book of Jonah

II. The Songs of Israel

   A. The Book of Psalms

1. Prayers that are filled with emotions

2. Poetry that appeals to the imagination

3. Categories of Psalms

   a. Psalms of Lament

   b. Psalms of Praise

      "Praise the LORD, all you nations!
         Give glory, all you peoples!
      The LORD's love for us is strong;
         the LORD is faithful forever.
      Hallelujah!" *(Ps 117)*

   c. Psalms of Thanksgiving

      "You changed my mourning into dancing;
         you took off my sackcloth
         and clothed me with gladness.
      With my whole being I sing
         endless praise to you.
      O LORD, my God,
         forever will I give you thanks." *(Ps 30:12-13)*

   d. Psalms of Trust

   e. Royal Psalms

      " 'I myself have installed my king
         on Zion, my holy mountain.'
      I will proclaim the decree of the LORD,
         who said to me, 'You are my son;
         today I am your father.
      Only ask it of me,
         and I will make your inheritance the nations,
         your possession the ends of the earth.' " *(Ps 2:6-8)*

f. Wisdom Psalms

> "Happy those who do not follow
>   the counsel of the wicked,
> Nor go the way of sinners,
>   nor sit in company with scoffers.
> Rather, the law of the LORD is their joy;
>   God's law they study day and night.
> They are like a tree
>   planted near streams of water,
>   that yields its fruit in season." *(Ps 1:1-3)*

4. The Five Books of Psalms

   a. Pss 1–41

   b. Pss 42–72

   c. Pss 73–89

   d. Pss 90–106

   e. Pss 107–150

> "Praise God in his holy sanctuary;
>   give praise in the mighty dome of heaven.
> Give praise for his mighty deeds,
>   praise him for his great majesty.
> Give praise with blasts upon the horn,
>   praise him with harp and lyre.
> Give praise with tambourines and dance,
>   praise him with flutes and strings.
> Give praise with crashing symbols,
>   praise him with sounding cymbals.
> Let everything that has breath
>   give praise to the LORD!
> Hallelujah!" *(Ps 150)*

B. The Song of Songs

"Set me as a seal on your heart,
   as a seal on your arm;
For stern as death is love,
   relentless as the nether world is devotion;
   its flames are a blazing fire.
Deep waters cannot quench love,
   nor floods sweep it away." *(Song 8:6-7)*

LECTURE 6—THE WRITINGS: ISRAEL'S WISDOM TRADITION

I. The Wisdom Writings

   A. Job, Proverbs, Ecclesiastes, Wisdom, and Sirach

   B. The Wisdom of Egypt and Mesopotamia

   C. "The beginning of wisdom is fear of the Lord."

   D. Solomon: inspiration and patron of Israel's wisdom

   E. Priests, Prophets, and Sages

   F. The sources of Israel's wisdom

      1. Reflecting on God's revelation

      2. Meditating on human experience

   G. Wisdom leads to a good life

II. The Book of Job

    A. Innocent suffering: faith's most perplexing problem

    B. The traditional answer: suffering is caused by sin

    C. God's answer: eternal questions of the universe

    D. Job's humble faith

> "Then Job answered the LORD and said:
> I know that you can do all things,
>   and that no purpose of yours can be hindered.
> I have dealt with great things that I do not understand;
>   things too wonderful for me, which I cannot know.
> I had heard of you by word of mouth,
>   but now my eye has seen you.
> Therefore I disown what I have said,
>   and repent in dust and ashes." *(Job 42:1-6)*

III. The Book of Proverbs

    A. Practical advice and basic values

    B. Rooted in relationship with God

> "The beginning of wisdom is the fear of the LORD, and knowledge of the Holy One is understanding." *(Prov 9:10)*

C. Guidelines for reading Proverbs

    1. Designed to give brief, practical advice

    2. Phrased to be catchy and easily learned

    3. Intended to be read together and balanced by one another

    4. Reflect the practices of an ancient culture

    5. Use of metaphor, exaggeration, and other techniques to express truth

IV. The Book of Ecclesiastes

A. A book of reflections by Qoheleth

B. Theme: "All things are vanity."

C. Nothing in this life can satisfy the longings of the human heart

"The last word, when all is heard: Fear God and keep his commandments, for this is man's all; because God will bring to judgment every work, with all its hidden qualities, whether good or bad." *(Eccl 12:13-14)*

V. The Book of Wisdom

A. Wis 1–5—Teachings on eternal life

"But the just live forever,
  and in the LORD is their recompense,
  and the thought of them is with the Most High.
Therefore shall they receive the splendid crown,
  the beauteous diadem, from the hand of the LORD—
For he shall shelter them with his right hand,
  and protect them with his arm." *(Wis 5:15-16)*

B. Wis 6–9—Praise of wisdom

"She is an aura of the might of God
  and a pure effusion of the glory of the Almighty. . . .
For she is the refulgence of eternal light,
  the spotless mirror of the power of God,
  the image of his goodness.
And she, who is one, can do all things,
  and renews everything while herself perduring;
And passing into holy souls from age to age,
  she produces friends of God and prophets." *(Wis 7:25-27)*

C. Wis 10–19—God's wisdom guiding Israel in Egypt

VI. The Book of Sirach

A. Sir 1–43—Practical moral instructions

B. Sir 44–50—God's great deeds throughout the history of Israel

LECTURE 7—THE PROPHETIC BOOKS: CHALLENGING THE TIMES

I.   The Role of the Prophets

   A. The call to conversion

   B. One who speaks for God

II. Development of the prophetic ministry

   A. Samuel, Nathan, Ahijah

   B. Elijah and Elisha

III. The Classical Prophets

   A. The major prophets—Isaiah, Jeremiah (Lamentations and Baruch), Ezekiel, and Daniel

   B. The twelve minor prophets—Hosea, Joel, Amos, Obadiah, Jonah, Micah, Nahum, Habakkuk, Zephaniah, Haggai, Zechariah, and Malachi.

IV.   The Prophets and Israel's Monarchy [refer to chart]

V.   Qualities of Authentic Prophecy

    A. Fulfillment of prophecy

    B. Content of the message in conformity with the covenant

    C. Courage in proclaiming the message

    D. Personal certitude about the prophetic call

VI.   The Call of the Prophets

VII. Faithfulness to the Covenant

    A. Worship of Yahweh alone

    B. Justice toward others

VIII. The Language of the Prophets

    A. Threats and promises

    B. Imaginative language

    C. Acted out prophecy

IX. The Pre-exilic Prophets

    A. Amos

> "I hate, I spurn your feasts,
>   I take no pleasure in your solemnities;
> Your cereal offerings I will not accept,
>   nor consider your stall-fed peace offerings.
> Away with your noisy songs!
>   I will not listen to the melodies of your harps.
> But if you would offer me holocausts,
>   then let justice surge like water,
>   and goodness like an unfailing stream." *(Amos 5:21-24)*

    B. Hosea

> "I will espouse you to me forever:
>   I will espouse you in right and in justice,
>   in love and in mercy;

I will espouse you in fidelity,
　　and you shall know the LORD." *(Hos 2:21-22)*

C. Isaiah

"Holy, holy, holy is the LORD of hosts! . . .
　　All the earth is filled with his glory." *(Isa 6:3)*

D. Micah

"With what shall I come before the LORD,
　　and bow before God most high?
Shall I come before him with holocausts,
　　with calves a year old?
Will the LORD be pleased with thousands of rams,
　　with myriad streams of oil?
Shall I give my first-born for my crime,
　　the fruit of my body for the sin of my soul?
You have been told, O man, what is good,
　　and what the LORD requires of you:
Only to do the right and to love goodness,
　　and to walk humbly with your God." *(Mic 6:6-8)*

E. Jeremiah

"The days are coming, says the LORD, when I will make a new covenant with the house of Israel and the house of Judah. It will not be like the covenant I made with their fathers the day I took them by the hand to lead them forth from the land of Egypt; for they broke my covenant and I had to show myself their master, says the LORD. But this is the covenant which I will make with the house of Israel after those days, says the LORD. I will place my law within them, and write it upon their hearts; I will be their God, and they shall be my people. No longer will they have need to teach their friends and kinsmen how to know the LORD. All, from least to greatest, shall know me, says the Lord, for I will forgive their evildoing and remember their sin no more." *(Jer 31:31-34)*

KINGS AND *PROPHETS*

	ISRAEL		JUDAH	
	Saul		*Samuel*	
B.C.E. 1000	David		*Nathan*	
	Solomon		*Ahijah*	
	ISRAEL		**JUDAH**	
	Jeroboam I		Rehoboam	
900	Baasha		Asa	
	Omri		Jehoshaphat	
	Ahab	*Elijah*		
	Jehu	*Elisha*	Jehoash	
800			Amaziah	
	Jeroboam II	*Amos*	Uzziah	
		Hosea	Jotham	*Isaiah*
	Menahem		Ahaz	*Micah*
	Hoshea			
	FALL OF SAMARIA			
700			Hezekiah	
			Manasseh	
			Josiah	*Zephaniah*
				Jeremiah
				Nahum
			Jehoiakim	*Habbakuk*
600			Zedekiah	
			FALL OF JERUSALEM	
			EXILE	*Ezekiel*
				2 Isaiah

LECTURE 8—THE PROPHETIC BOOKS: HOPING IN THE FUTURE

I. Words of Hope in the Midst of Exile

"For I know well the plans I have in mind for you, says the LORD, plans for your welfare, not for woe! plans to give you a future full of hope." *(Jer 29:11)*

II. Foundational Elements of the Covenant Seemed Destroyed

   A. Davidic Kingship

   B. Land of Israel

   C. Temple, Priesthood, and Sacrifice

III. Ezekiel

   A. A prophet in Exile

   B. The Book of Ezekiel

      1. Ezek 1–32—Warnings of Destruction

      2. Ezek 33–48—Promise after Destruction

C. Hope for Restoration

"I will give you a new heart and place a new spirit within you." *(Ezek 36:26)*

"I will put sinews upon you, make flesh grow over you, cover you with skin, and put spirit in you so that you may come to life and know that I am the LORD." *(Ezek 37:6)*

D. Foundational Elements of the Covenant to be Restored

1. Davidic kingship

   "My servant David shall be prince over them, and there shall be one shepherd for them all." *(Ezek 37:24)*

2. Land of Israel

   "They shall live on the land which I gave to my servant Jacob, the land where their fathers lived; they shall live on it forever." *(Ezek 37:25)*

3. Temple in Jerusalem

   "My dwelling shall be with them; I will be their God, and they shall be my people. Thus the nations shall know that it is I, the LORD, who make Israel holy, when my sanctuary shall be set up among them forever." *(Ezek 37:27-28)*

IV. Deutero-Isaiah *(Isa 40–55)*

A. A new exodus

B. A book of consolation

"Comfort, give comfort to my people,
    says your God.
Speak tenderly to Jerusalem, and proclaim to her
    that her service is at an end,
    her guilt is expiated;
Indeed, she has received from the hand of the LORD
    double for all her sins.
        A voice cries out:
In the desert prepare the way of the LORD!
Make straight in the wasteland a highway for our God!"

(Isa 40:1-3)

V.   Haggai and Zechariah

A. The future temple

"Greater will be the future glory of this house
    than the former, says the LORD of hosts;
And in this place I will give peace,
    says the LORD of hosts." *(Hag 2:9)*

B. Restored Jerusalem

"Many peoples and strong nations shall come to seek the
LORD of hosts in Jerusalem and to implore the favor of the
LORD. Thus says the LORD of hosts: In those days ten men
of every nationality, speaking different tongues, shall take
hold, yes, take hold of every Jew by the edge of his garment
and say, 'Let us go with you, for we have heard that God is
with you.'" *(Zech 8:22-23)*

VI.   Prophetic Hope is Deferred but not Abandoned

  A. Hope for a future king, restored land, and renewed temple is oriented toward the more distant future

  B. Prophetic hope is universalized

VII. Trito-Isaiah *(Isa 56–66)*

  A. Wondrous future intervention of God

  B. Hope for restored Jerusalem

  "Lo, I am about to create new heavens
    and a new earth;
  The things of the past shall not be remembered
    or come to mind.
  Instead, there shall always be rejoicing and happiness
    in what I create;
  For I create Jerusalem to be a joy
    and its people to be a delight." *(Isa 65:17-18)*

VIII. Malachi

  "Lo, I am sending my messenger
    to prepare the way before me;

And suddenly there will come to the temple
the LORD whom you seek,
And the messenger of the covenant whom you desire.
Yes, he is coming, says the LORD of hosts." *(Mal 3:1)*

IX. Characteristics of Apocalyptic literature

    A. Originates in a time of crisis in order to inspire hope.

    B. Marked by confidence that God will destroy evil and reward the faithful with God's kingdom.

    C. Describes disturbances in the heavens and on the earth heralding the coming of the "Day of the Lord."

    D. Uses symbolic names, numbers, and creatures to convey its message.

X. Joel

    A. The Day of the Lord

    B. A spirit of prophecy on all people

"Then afterward I will pour out
  my spirit upon all mankind.
Your sons and daughters shall prophesy,
  your old men shall dream dreams,
  your young men shall see visions;
Even upon the servants and the handmaids,
  in those days, I will pour out my spirit.
And I will work wonders in the heavens and on the earth,
  blood, fire, and columns of smoke;
The sun will be turned to darkness,
  and the moon to blood,
At the coming of the day of the LORD,
  the great and terrible day.
Then everyone shall be rescued
  who calls on the name of the LORD." *(Joel 3:1-5)*

XI. Daniel

A. Stories of God's salvation in time of persecution

B. Visions of the world empires

XII. Fuller Meaning of Prophecy Anticipates the Messiah and the Reign of God

A. A humble saving king

"Rejoice heartily, O daughter Zion,
  shout for joy, O daughter Jerusalem$_1$

See, your king shall come to you;
  a just savior is he,
Meek and riding on an ass." *(Zech 9:9)*

"They shall look on him whom they have thrust through, and they shall mourn for him as one mourns for an only son." *(Zech 12:10)*

B. The Suffering Servant

"But he was pierced for our offenses,
  crushed for our sins. . . .
But the LORD laid upon him
  the guilt of us all" *(Isa 53:5-6)*

"Because of his affliction
  he shall see the light in fullness of days;
Through his suffering, my servant shall justify many,
  and their guilt he shall bear.
Therefore I will give him his portion among the great,
  and he shall divide the spoils with the mighty,
Because he surrendered himself to death
  and was counted among the wicked;
And he shall take away the sins of many,
  and win pardon for their offenses." *(Isa 53:11-12)*

XIII. Conclusion

QUESTIONS FOR STUDY AND DISCUSSION

1. The Old Testament is the story of the ancestors of our faith.

   a. What do you know about the ancestors of your family?
   Came from Poland - Interesting family histories

   b. Why are the stories of your ancestors important to you?
   - Gives meaning to my life - If I were adopted and didn't have a clue about my family background I'd feel los

2. Genesis 1 and 2 are stories of God's creation culminating in the creation of human persons.

   a. Read Genesis 1:27. What does it mean to you that man and woman are created in the image of God? *Created c intelligence, soul, spirit, ability to make judgeme*
   goodness b. Read Genesis 2:7. What do you think it means to say that humankind was created from the clay of the earth and the breath of God? What does this say about our human nature?

   - We are part animal - like all the other animals of the earth but yet we have spirits, soul, intellect - we don't just follow our instincts like other animals

3. The colorful stories of Genesis express God's desire for humankind and the effects of human choice.

   a. In what ways is the account of Adam and Eve the story of each of us? *Each of us is given the ability to make choices - Each of us make wrong decision sometimes in our lives*

   b. How do the stories of Creation and the Fall form a preamble for all of salvation history?

   It is what we experience in today's world - We are created in all goodness - innocent children and we enter a world both good but also sinful c corruption - It is our task to bring about good in the world

74

– We are still given a choice –
We can choose to Be good
and follow God's way or
we can choose to be sinful –

4. Jacob, whose name became Israel, had a dream in which he saw a stairway linking heaven and earth. Read Genesis 28:12-17.

a. What are the promises God made to Jacob (Israel)?

— land to his descendants — many descendants

b. Is there anything or any place in your life that represents a link between heaven and earth? — My spiritual

— Basilica —

life — My artistic endeavours however simple they are. — Walking in nature — Just talking to God in Silence   Word of God - Scriptures

5. A summary of the Pentateuch may be found in Exodus 6:2-8.

What are the promises God makes to the Israelites in this formative stage of their history? — To rescue them from slavery from Egypt — To have their own land

— To make himself known to the Israelites as the "Lord" their God —

- Shows his goodness to the Israelites

6. In every age God's people would renew the covenant with word and sacrifice. Read Exodus 24:3-8.

"We will obey the Lord and do everything he has commanded

a. What is the word that Moses read at Sinai?

book of the Covenant   Lord's commands

b. Describe the sacrifice he offered.

Cattle — ½ in bowls ½ thrown against altar.

c. How is God's covenant renewed today in word and sacrifice?

— Jesus sacrificed himself for all mankind so that we no longer have to kill animals as sacrifices — He became the sacrificial lamb —

Sacrament of the Holy Eucharist —
— Renew ourselves in faith —
                                    ∴ Mass

tabernacle

4 a   " through you and your
descendants I will bless all nations"
- Coming of Jesus forshadowed?
- That God would not leave him
  6

*Note: Some study questions deepen your understanding of what was learned in the previous lecture; other questions anticipate the material to be learned in the next lecture.

7. a. Read Numbers 14:1-10. Why do the people grumble and rebel on their journey to the promised land?

   b. What experiences in your own life are similar to those of Israel in the wilderness?

   c. Read Deuteronomy 8:2-5. Why does God allow Israel to experience hunger and affliction during their desert journey?

8. a. Read Deuteronomy 30:11-14. Where do God's people find the will of God? How does this assure you in your search to discover God's will in the circumstances of your life?

   b. Read Deuteronomy 30:15-20. What does it mean for each generation of Israelites to "choose life"?

9. Read Judges 2:10-23. This is a brief outline of the cyclical pattern repeated throughout the book of Judges.

   Give an example of how you experience this pattern of sin, punishment, repentance, and deliverance in your own life or in our society.

10. Read 1 Samuel 8 and 12. These chapters contain arguments for and against an earthly king to reign over Israel.

   a. What reasons do the people give for wanting a king to rule them? *wanted a nation - temporal pow*

   b. What are the principal reasons for opposing the monarchy in Israel?
   – enslavement
   Kings would take control
   of people -
   – would the king be
   faithful to the covenant

11. God made an everlasting covenant with King David through his prophet Nathan. Read 2 Samuel 7.

   a. What does God promise King David by giving him a "house"?
   lineage descendants right down to christ

   b. Why do you think God did not allow David to build the Temple?

   c. Where do you find the dwelling of God: tent, temple, home, or family?

12. Read 1 Kings 8. This chapter describes the dedication of the Temple in Jerusalem and the prayer of King Solomon.

   a. In what ways do the Temple and the ark connect God's people to the covenant made with Moses on Mount Sinai?

   b. In what ways does the Temple connect God's people to the covenant made with King David?

   c. What are some of the ways King Solomon expects the Temple to be a sign of God's continuing faithfulness for the people?

→ House of Israel - the chosen people

13. a. Read Nehemiah 8. This gathering marks the culmination of Israel's restoration after the Exile.

   Why do you think the people wept when Ezra read to them from the Law of Moses? Why did Ezra tell them to rejoice and celebrate instead?

   b. Read Nehemiah 9. This ceremony of solemn penance culminates in the prayer of Ezra.

   What are some of the ways God has kept the covenant with Israel? What are some of the ways Israel has been disloyal to the covenant?

14. Read the Book of Ruth. In this short story, a foreign Moabite woman is joined by marriage to the people of Israel.

   a. Which qualities of Ruth do you most admire?

   b. How is God's care demonstrated throughout the story?

   c. How would this story be challenging to its readers in Israel?

15. Read Psalm 103. The psalmist gives praise for God's presence and action in the world.

   a. What are some of the psalmist's reasons for gratitude that are particularly striking to you?

   b. What could help you recognize God's activity more consciously?

16. Solomon is the patron of Israel's wisdom writings. Read 1 Kings 3:1-15.

   a. What is the gift which King Solomon requested from God?
      wisdom

   b. Why was God so pleased with Solomon's request?
      didn't ask for riches etc.

   c. What gift could you ask from God that would be most appropriate to the circumstances of your life?

17. a. Read Job 1. In this dramatic story, the author explored the mystery of human suffering. Why does God allow Job to suffer?

    b. Read Job 31. What is the basis of Job's case as he examines his life and pleads his innocence before God?

    c. Do you feel an empathy with Job? Why?

18. Read Proverbs 31:10-31. This poem reflects the image of one who embodies God's wisdom in an authentic, human, and fully integrated way.

    a. What are the characteristics that make her praiseworthy before God?

    b. Is this image of the wise person realistic or too idealistic? Why?

    c. What qualities of the wise person do you most desire?

19. Read Deuteronomy 18:9-22. Here the writer describes the role of the prophet in Israel.

  a. How are the prophets of Israel different from the seers of other nations?

  b. Moses promises Israel "a prophet like me." What characteristics of Moses make him a model for all prophets?

20. Read 1 Kings 19. The prophet Elijah escapes from persecution, flees to the desert, encounters God on Mount Sinai, and appoints a successor.

  a. How is Moses' encounter with God on the mountain different from that of Elijah?

  b. What parallels do you see in the experiences of Moses and Elijah?

  c. What does the "tiny whispering sound" teach you about seeking God's will?

21. Compare the call of Moses (Exod 3:1-14), Isaiah (Isa 6:1-13), and Jeremiah (Jer 1:4-9).

   a. What similarities do you notice in each call narrative?

   b. What are the unique characteristics about each of the three accounts?

22. Read Isaiah 7:10-16; 9:1-6; and 11:1-9, prophecies of the coming Immanuel. Isaiah was proclaiming that God would rescue the people of Judah in their distress through an ideal king. A partial fulfillment of this prophecy was seen in the reign of King Hezekiah, a reforming king from the line of David.

   a. How have these prophecies taken on fuller meaning in later periods of history?

   b. What are the qualities of God's Kingdom as described in these prophecies?

   c. When and where have you heard these prophecies proclaimed?

23. Read Isaiah 55:6-11, a message of hope for the exiles in Babylon.

    a. In what ways do you think you are being challenged to "seek the Lord"?

    b. How do verses 8-9 encourage you in your frustrations when attempting to understand the difficulties of life?

    c. How is the Word of God like rain and snow in your life?

24. Read Daniel 7. As an example of Jewish apocalyptic literature, it is marked by highly symbolic and unusual imagery. The four beasts represent four kingdoms of the world.

    a. Daniel is terrified by what he sees in his dream. What do you find frightening about this vision?

    b. As an apocalyptic passage, these verses are intended to inspire courage and hope during a period of crisis. What do you find hopeful here?

NOTES